Usborne
Illustrated
Nursery
Rhymes

Usborne
Illustrated
Nursery
Rhymes

Chosen by Felicity Brooks

Illustrated by Laura Rigo

Designed by
Nancy Leschnikoff,
Catherine-Anne MacKinnon
and Mary Cartwright

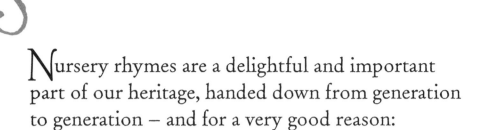

Nursery rhymes are a delightful and important part of our heritage, handed down from generation to generation – and for a very good reason:

Reciting and singing rhymes is a great way to support children's language learning, because listening to rhymes again and again allows them to develop an understanding of the rhythms of language and the way that words work. This not only helps little children learn to talk, but is also a vital pre-reading skill. Many nursery rhymes and sayings also introduce early learning concepts such as counting, time, the weather and the days of the week in an entertaining way.

I hope you have as much enjoyment sharing these beautifully illustrated rhymes with your child as I had choosing them.

Felicity Brooks

Humpty Dumpty

Humpty Dumpty sat on a wall,
Humpty Dumpty had a great fall;
All the King's horses and all the King's men
Couldn't put Humpty together again.

Sing a Song o' Sixpence

Sing a song o' sixpence,
A pocket full of rye;
Four-and-twenty blackbirds,
Baked in a pie.

~ 6 ~

When the pie was opened,
The birds began to sing;
Wasn't that a dainty dish
To set before the King?

The King was in his counting-house,
Counting out his money;
The Queen was in the parlour,
Eating bread and honey.

The maid was in the garden,
Hanging out the clothes,
When down came a blackbird
And pecked off her nose.

Mary, Mary, Quite Contrary

Mary, Mary, quite contrary,
How does your garden grow?
With silver bells,
And cockle shells,
And pretty maids all in a row.

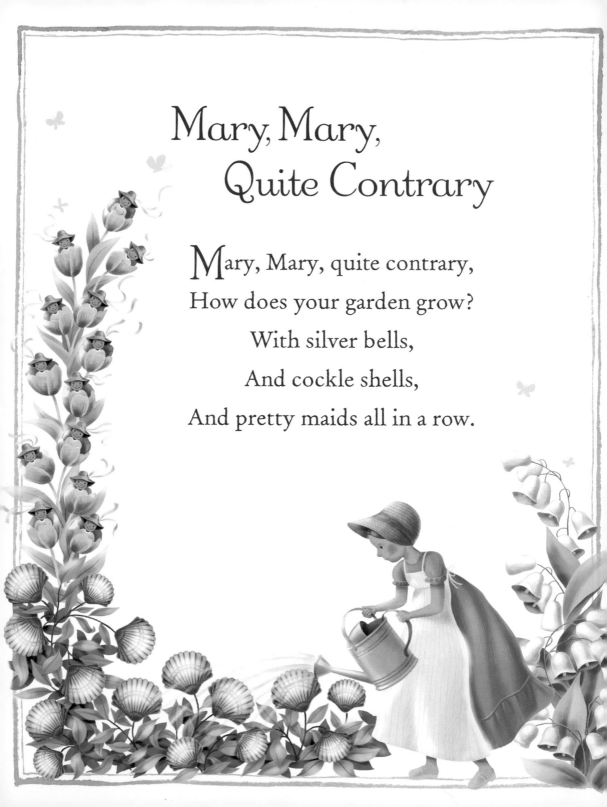

Here we go Gathering Nuts in May

Here we go gathering nuts in May,
Nuts in May, nuts in May,
Here we go gathering nuts in May,
On a cold and frosty morning.

Hey Diddle, Diddle

Hey diddle, diddle,
The cat and the fiddle,
The cow jumped over the moon;
The little dog laughed
To see such fun,
And the dish ran away
With the spoon.

Jack and Jill

Jack and Jill,
went up the hill,
To fetch a pail of water.
Jack fell down,
and broke his crown,
And Jill came tumbling after.

Baa, Baa, Black Sheep

Baa, baa, black sheep,
Have you any wool?
Yes, sir, yes, sir,
Three bags full;

One for the master,
And one for the dame,
And one for the little boy
Who lives down the lane.

Little Bo-peep

Little Bo-peep has lost her sheep,
And doesn't know where to find them;
Leave them alone, and they'll come home,
Wagging their tails behind them.

Here we go Round the Mulberry Bush

Here we go round the mulberry bush,
The mulberry bush, the mulberry bush;
Here we go round the mulberry bush,
On a cold and frosty morning.

This is the way we wash our face,
Wash our face, wash our face;
This is the way we wash our face,
On a cold and frosty morning.

This is the way we brush our hair,
Brush our hair, brush our hair;
This is the way we brush our hair,
On a cold and frosty morning.

This is the way we put on our clothes,
Put on our clothes, put on our clothes;
This is the way we put on our clothes,
On a cold and frosty morning.

This is the way we brush our teeth,
Brush our teeth, brush our teeth;
This is the way we brush our teeth,
On a cold and frosty morning.

Lucy Locket

Lucy Locket lost her pocket,
Kitty Fisher found it;
But not a penny was there in it,
Only ribbon around it.

Georgie Porgie

Georgie Porgie, pudding and pie,
Kissed the girls and made them cry;
When the boys came out to play,
Georgie Porgie ran away.

Little Boy Blue

Little boy blue,
Come blow your horn,
The sheep's in the meadow,
The cow's in the corn;
But where is the boy
Who looks after the sheep?
He's under a haystack,
Fast asleep.
Will you wake him?
No, not I,
For if I do,
He's sure to cry.

See-saw, Margery Daw

See-saw, Margery Daw,
Johnny shall have a new master;
He shall have but a penny a day,
Because he can't work any faster.

Jack be Nimble

Jack be nimble,
Jack be quick,
Jack jump over
The candlestick.

Jack Sprat

Jack Sprat could eat no fat,
His wife could eat no lean,
And so between them both, you see,
They licked the platter clean.

Peter, Peter, Pumpkin-eater

Peter, Peter, pumpkin-eater,
Had a wife and couldn't keep her;
He put her in a pumpkin shell,
And there he kept her very well.

Peter, Peter, pumpkin-eater,
Had another, and didn't love her;
Peter learned to read and spell,
And then he loved her very well.

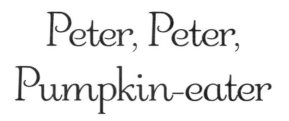

Cock-a-doodle-doo!

Cock-a-doodle-doo!
My dame has lost her shoe,
My master's lost his fiddling stick,
And doesn't know what to do.

Cock-a-doodle-doo!
What is my dame to do?
Till master finds his fiddling stick,
She'll dance without her shoe.

Cock-a-doodle-doo!
My dame has found her shoe,
And master's found his fiddling stick,
Sing cock-a-doodle-doo!

Cock-a-doodle-doo!
My dame shall dance with you,
While master fiddles his fiddling stick
For dame and doodle-doo.

What are Little Girls made of?

What are little girls made of?
Sugar and spice
And all things nice;
That's what little girls are made of.

What are Little Boys made of?

What are little boys made of?
Slugs and snails
And puppy-dogs' tails;
That's what little boys are made of.

There was a Little Girl

There was a little girl, and she had a little curl
Right in the middle of her forehead;
And when she was good, she was very, very good,
But when she was bad, she was horrid.

Yankee Doodle

Yankee Doodle came to town,
Riding on a pony;
He stuck a feather in his cap
And called it macaroni.

Gregory Griggs, Gregory Griggs

Gregory Griggs, Gregory Griggs
Had twenty-seven different wigs.
He wore them up, he wore them down
To please the people of the town;
He wore them east, he wore them west,
But he never could tell which he loved the best.

Hickory, Dickory, Dock!

Hickory, dickory, dock!
The mouse ran up the clock.
The clock struck one,
The mouse ran down,
Hickory, dickory, dock!

The Grand Old Duke of York

The grand old Duke of York,
He had ten thousand men;
He marched them up
To the top of the hill,
And he marched them down again.

And when they were up, they were up,
And when they were down, they were down,
And when they were only half-way up,
They were neither up nor down.

Ride a Cock-horse

Ride a cock-horse to Banbury Cross,
To see a fine lady upon a white horse;
With rings on her fingers and bells on her toes,
She shall have music wherever she goes.

Curly Locks, Curly Locks

Curly Locks, Curly Locks,
Wilt thou be mine?
Thou shalt not wash dishes
Nor yet feed the swine,
But sit on a cushion
And sew a fine seam,
And feed upon strawberries,
Sugar and cream.

Simple Simon

Simple Simon met a pieman
Going to the fair;
Said Simple Simon to the pieman,
"Let me taste your ware."

Said the pieman unto Simon,
"Show me first your penny,"
Said Simple Simon to the pieman,
"Sir, I haven't any."

Simple Simon went a-fishing,
For to catch a whale;
But all the water that he got
Was in his mother's pail.

Simple Simon went to look
If plums grew on a thistle;
He pricked his fingers very much,
Which made poor Simon whistle.

Three Blind Mice

Three blind mice, three blind mice,
See how they run! See how they run!
They all ran after the farmer's wife,
Who cut off their tails with a carving knife,
Did ever you see such a thing in your life,
As three blind mice?

Hark, Hark

Hark, hark,
The dogs do bark,
The beggars are coming to town;
Some in rags,
And some in jags,
And one in a velvet gown.

Ding, Dong, Bell

Ding, dong, bell,
Pussy's in the well.
Who put her in?
Little Johnny Green.
Who pulled her out?
Little Tommy Stout.
What a naughty boy was that,
To try to drown poor pussy cat,
Who never did any harm,
But killed all the mice in his father's barn.

Dance to your Daddy

Dance to your daddy,
My little babby,
Dance to your daddy,
My little lamb.
You shall have a fishy
In a little dishy;
You shall have a fishy,
When the boat comes in.

Goosey, Goosey Gander

Goosey, goosey gander,
Whither shall I wander?
Upstairs and downstairs
And in my lady's chamber.
There I met an old man
Who would not say his prayers;
I took him by the left leg
And threw him down the stairs.

Hickety, Pickety, my Black Hen

Hickety, pickety, my black hen,
She lays eggs for gentlemen;
Gentlemen come every day
To see what my black hen doth lay.

The Lion and the Unicorn

The lion and the unicorn
Were fighting for the crown;
The lion beat the unicorn
All around the town.

Some gave them white bread,
And some gave them brown;
Some gave them plum-cake,
And drummed them out of town.

The Man in the Moon

The man in the moon
Came down too soon,
And asked his way to Norwich;
He went by the south,
And burnt his mouth
Eating cold pease porridge.

Hot Cross Buns!

Hot cross buns!
Hot cross buns!
One a penny, two a penny,
Hot cross buns!
If you have no daughters,
Give them to your sons;
One a penny, two a penny,
Hot cross buns!

Pease Pudding Hot

Pease pudding hot,
Pease pudding cold,
Pease pudding in the pot,
Nine days old.

Some like it hot,
Some like it cold,
Some like it in the pot,
Nine days old.

Red Sky at Night

Red sky at night,
Shepherd's delight.
Red sky in the morning,
Shepherd's warning.

Early to Bed

Early to bed and early to rise
Makes a man healthy,
Wealthy and wise.

There was a Crooked Man

There was a crooked man,
And he walked a crooked mile,
And he found a crooked sixpence
Upon a crooked stile;
He bought a crooked cat,
Which caught a crooked mouse,
And they all lived together
In a little crooked house.

A Farmer went Trotting

A farmer went trotting upon his grey mare,
Bumpety, bumpety, bump!
With his daughter behind him so rosy and fair,
Lumpety, lumpety, lump!

A raven cried, "Croak!" and they all tumbled down,
Bumpety, bumpety, bump!
The mare broke her knees and the farmer his crown,
Lumpety, lumpety, lump!

The mischievous raven flew laughing away,
Bumpety, bumpety, bump!
And vowed he would serve them the same the next day,
Lumpety, lumpety, lump!

Lavender's Blue

Lavender's blue, dilly, dilly,
Lavender's green,
When I am King, dilly, dilly,
You shall be Queen.

Call up your men, dilly, dilly,
Set them to work,
Some to the plough, dilly, dilly,
Some to the cart.

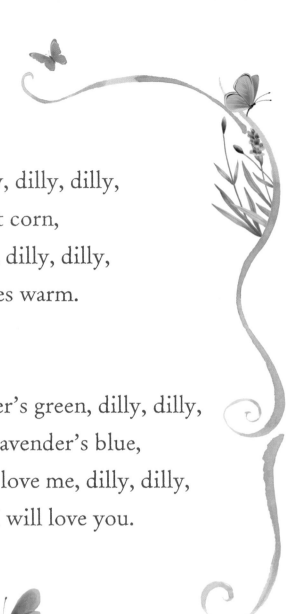

Some to make hay, dilly, dilly,
Some to cut corn,
While you and I, dilly, dilly,
Keep ourselves warm.

Lavender's green, dilly, dilly,
Lavender's blue,
If you love me, dilly, dilly,
I will love you.

Rub-a-dub-dub

Rub-a-dub-dub,
Three men in a tub,
And who do you think they be?
The butcher, the baker,
The candlestick-maker,
So turn out the knaves, all three.

Pat-a-cake, Pat-a-cake

Pat-a-cake, pat-a-cake, baker's man,
Bake me a cake just as fast as you can;
Pat it and prick it, and mark it with B,
And put it in the oven for baby and me.

Cobbler, Cobbler

Cobbler, cobbler, mend my shoe,
Get it done by half-past two;
Half-past two is much too late,
Get it done by half-past eight.

London Bridge

London Bridge is falling down,
Falling down, falling down;
London Bridge is falling down,
My fair lady.

Build it up with wood and clay,
Wood and clay, wood and clay;
Build it up with wood and clay,
My fair lady.

Wood and clay will wash away,
Wash away, wash away;
Wood and clay will wash away,
My fair lady.

Build it up with bricks and mortar,
Bricks and mortar, bricks and mortar;
Build it up with bricks and mortar,
My fair lady.

Bricks and mortar will not stay,
Will not stay, will not stay;
Bricks and mortar will not stay,
My fair lady.

Build it up with iron and steel,
Iron and steel, iron and steel;
Build it up with iron and steel,
My fair lady.

Iron and steel will bend and bow,
Bend and bow, bend and bow;
Iron and steel will bend and bow,
My fair lady.

Build it up with silver and gold,
Silver and gold, silver and gold;
Build it up with silver and gold,
My fair lady.

Silver and gold will be stolen away,
Stolen away, stolen away;
Silver and gold will be stolen away,
My fair lady.

Set a man to watch all night,
Watch all night, watch all night;
Set a man to watch all night,
My fair lady.

Old King Cole

Old King Cole
Was a merry old soul,
And a merry old soul was he;
He called for his pipe,
And he called for his bowl,
And he called for his fiddlers three.

Now, every fiddler, he had a fiddle,
And a very fine fiddle had he;
Oh, there's none so rare
As can compare
With King Cole and his fiddlers three.

Little Miss Muffet

Little Miss Muffet
Sat on a tuffet,
Eating her curds and whey;
Along came a spider,
Who sat down beside her,
And frightened Miss Muffet away.

Oranges and Lemons

Oranges and lemons,
Say the bells of St Clement's.

You owe me five farthings,
Say the bells of St Martin's.

When will you pay me?
Say the bells of Old Bailey.

When I grow rich,
Say the bells of Shoreditch.

When will that be?
Say the bells of Stepney.

I'm sure I don't know,
Says the great bell at Bow.

Pop goes the Weasel!

Up and down the City Road,
In and out the Eagle;
That's the way the money goes,
Pop goes the weasel!

Half a pound of tuppenny rice,
Half a pound of treacle;
That's the way the money goes,
Pop goes the weasel!

Every night when I get home
The monkey's on the table;
Take a stick and knock it off,
Pop goes the weasel!

Do you know the Muffin Man?

Do you know the muffin man,
The muffin man, the muffin man,
Do you know the muffin man,
Who lives in Drury Lane?

Yes, I know the muffin man,
The muffin man, the muffin man,
Yes, I know the muffin man,
Who lives in Drury Lane.

Tom, Tom, the Piper's Son

Tom, Tom, the piper's son,
Stole a pig and away he run;
The pig was eat and Tom was beat,
And Tom went howling down the street.

Betty Botter

Betty Botter bought some butter,
But, she said, this butter's bitter;
If I put it in my batter,
It will make my batter bitter,
But a bit of better butter,
That would make my batter better.
So she bought a bit of butter
Better than her bitter butter,
And she put it in her batter
And the batter was not bitter.
So t'was better Betty Botter
Bought a bit of better butter.

Peter Piper

Peter Piper picked a peck of pickled pepper;
A peck of pickled pepper Peter Piper picked;
If Peter Piper picked a peck of pickled pepper,
Where's the peck of pickled pepper Peter Piper picked?

Round and Round the Rugged Rock

Round and round the rugged rock
The ragged rascal ran.
How many R's are there in that?
Now tell me if you can.

Ring-a-ring o'Roses

Ring-a-ring o' roses,
A pocket full of posies,
A-tishoo! A-tishoo!
We all fall down.

The cows are in the meadow
Eating buttercups,
A-tishoo! A-tishoo!
We all jump up!

Polly put the Kettle on

Polly put the kettle on,
Polly put the kettle on,
Polly put the kettle on,
We'll all have tea.

Sukey take it off again,
Sukey take it off again,
Sukey take it off again,
They've all gone away.

Oh Dear, What can the Matter be?

Oh dear, what can the matter be?
Dear, dear, what can the matter be?
Oh dear, what can the matter be?
Johnny's so long at the fair.

He promised to buy me a fairing to please me,
And then for a kiss, oh, he vowed he would tease me!
He promised to buy me a bunch of blue ribbons
To tie up my bonny brown hair.

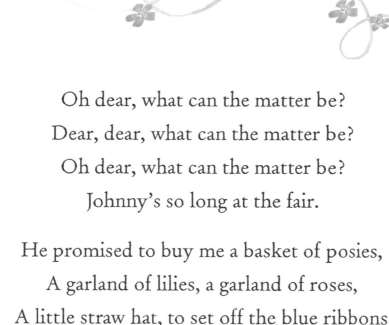

Oh dear, what can the matter be?
Dear, dear, what can the matter be?
Oh dear, what can the matter be?
Johnny's so long at the fair.

He promised to buy me a basket of posies,
A garland of lilies, a garland of roses,
A little straw hat, to set off the blue ribbons
That tie up my bonny brown hair.

O dear, what can the matter be?
Dear, dear, what can the matter be?
O dear, what can the matter be?
Johnny's so long at the fair.

The North Wind doth Blow

The north wind doth blow,

And we shall have snow,

And what will the robin do then, poor thing?

He'll sit in a barn

And keep himself warm,

And hide his head under his wing, poor thing!

Two Little Dicky Birds

Two little dicky birds
Sitting on a wall.
One named Peter,
One named Paul.
Fly away Peter!
Fly away Paul!
Come back Peter,
Come back Paul.

The Big Ship Sails
on the Alley-alley-oh

The big ship sails on the alley-alley-oh,
The alley-alley-oh, the alley-alley-oh.
The big ship sails on the alley-alley-oh,
On the last day of September.

The captain said it will never, never do,
Never, never do, never, never do.
The captain said it will never, never do,
On the last day of September.

The big ship sank to the bottom of the sea,
The bottom of the sea, the bottom of the sea.
The big ship sank to the bottom of the sea,
On the last day of September.

We all dip our heads in the deep blue sea,
The deep blue sea, the deep blue sea.
We all dip our heads in the deep blue sea,
On the last day of September.

Old Mother Hubbard

Old Mother Hubbard
Went to the cupboard,
To fetch her poor dog a bone;
But when she got there,
The cupboard was bare
And so the poor dog had none.

She went to the baker's
To buy him some bread;
But when she came back,
The poor dog was dead.

She went to the joiner's
To buy him a coffin;
But when she came back,
The poor dog was laughing.

She took a clean dish
To get him some tripe;
But when she came back,
He was smoking a pipe.

She went to the fishmonger's
To buy him some fish;
And when she came back,
He was washing the dish.

She went to the tailor's
To buy him a coat;
But when she came back,
He was riding a goat.

She went to the hatter's
To buy him a hat;
But when she came back
He was feeding the cat.

She went to the barber's
To buy him a wig;
But when she came back
He was dancing a jig.

She went to the cobbler's
To buy him some shoes;
But when she came back
He was reading the news.

She went to the seamstress
To buy him some linen;
But when she came back
The dog was a-spinning.

The dame made a curtsey,
The dog made a bow;
The dame said, "Your servant,"
The dog said, "Bow-wow."

One, Two, Three, Four, Five

One, two, three, four, five,
Once I caught a fish alive;
Six, seven, eight, nine, ten,
Then I let it go again.

Why did you let it go?
Because it bit my finger so.
Which finger did it bite?
This little finger on the right.

One Potato, Two Potato

One potato,

Two potato,

Three potato,

Four.

Five potato,

Six potato,

Seven potato,

More.

I'm the King of the Castle!

I'm the king of the castle!
Get down you dirty rascal!

Round and Round the Garden

Round and round the garden,
Like a teddy bear;
One step, two step,
Tickle you under there!

Row, Row, Row your Boat

Row, row, row your boat
Gently down the stream;
Merrily, merrily, merrily, merrily,
Life is but a dream.

This Little Piggy

This little piggy went to market,
This little piggy stayed at home,
This little piggy had roast beef,
This little piggy had none,
And this little piggy said,
"Wee, wee, wee, wee"
All the way home.

To Market, to Market

To market, to market, to buy a fat pig,
Home again, home again, jiggety-jig.

To market, to market, to buy a fat hog,
Home again, home again, jiggety-jog.

This is the Way the Ladies Ride

This is the way the ladies ride,
Trottity-trot, trottity-trot.
This is the way the ladies ride,
Trottity-trottity-trottity-TROT!

This is the way the gentlemen ride,
Gallopy-gallop, gallopy-gallop.
This is the way the gentlemen ride,
Gallopy-gallopy-gallopy-GALLOP!

This is the way the farmers ride,
Hobbledey-hoy, hobbledey-hoy.
This is the way the farmers ride,
Hobbledey-hobbledey-hobbledey-HOY!

The Queen of Hearts

The Queen of Hearts
She made some tarts,
All on a summer's day;
The Knave of Hearts
He stole the tarts,
And took them clean away.

The King of Hearts
Called for the tarts,
And beat the knave full sore;
The Knave of Hearts
Brought back the tarts,
And vowed he'd steal no more.

Little Jack Horner

Little Jack Horner
Sat in a corner,
Eating his Christmas pie;
He put in his thumb,
And pulled out a plum,
And said, "What a good boy am I!"

Monday's Child

Monday's child is fair of face,

Tuesday's child if full of grace,

Wednesday's child is full of woe,

Thursday's child has far to go,

Friday's child is loving and giving,

Saturday's child works hard for a living,

And the child that is born on the Sabbath day

Is bonny and blithe, and good and gay.

Solomon Grundy

Solomon Grundy,
Born on a Monday,
Christened on Tuesday,
Married on Wednesday,
Took ill on Thursday,
Worse on Friday,
Died on Saturday,
Buried on Sunday.
This is the end
Of Solomon Grundy.

Thirty Days hath September

Thirty days hath September,
April, June and November;
All the rest have thirty-one,
Except February alone,
And that has twenty-eight days clear,
And twenty-nine in each leap year.

The Farmer's in his Den

The farmer's in his den,
The farmer's in his den,
Eee-aye-adio,
The farmer's in his den.

The farmer wants a wife,
The farmer wants a wife,
Eee-aye-adio,
The farmer wants a wife.

The wife wants a child,
The wife wants a child,
Eee-aye-adio,
The wife wants a child.

The child wants a nurse,
The child wants a nurse,
Eee-aye-adio,
The child wants a nurse.

The nurse wants a dog,
The nurse wants a dog,
Eee-aye-adio,
The nurse wants a dog.

The dog wants a bone,
The dog wants a bone,
Eee-aye-adio,
The dog wants a bone.

We all pat the bone,
We all pat the bone,
Eee-aye-adio,
We all pat the bone.

Little Tommy Tucker

Little Tommy Tucker,
Sings for his supper:
What shall we give him?
White bread and butter.
How shall he cut it
Without e'er a knife?
How will he be married
Without e'er a wife?

Miss Polly had a Dolly

Miss Polly had a dolly
Who was sick, sick, sick.
So she called for the doctor
To come quick, quick, quick.
The doctor came
With his bag and his hat,
And he knocked on the door
With a rat-a-tat-tat.

He looked at the dolly
And he shook his head.
Then he said, "Miss Polly,
Put her straight to bed."
He wrote on a paper
For a pill, pill, pill;
"That'll make her better,
Yes, it will, will, will."

Incy Wincy Spider

Incy wincy spider
Climbed up the water spout.
Down came the rain and
Washed the spider out.

Out came the sunshine,
And dried up all the rain,
So incy wincy spider
Climbed up the spout again.

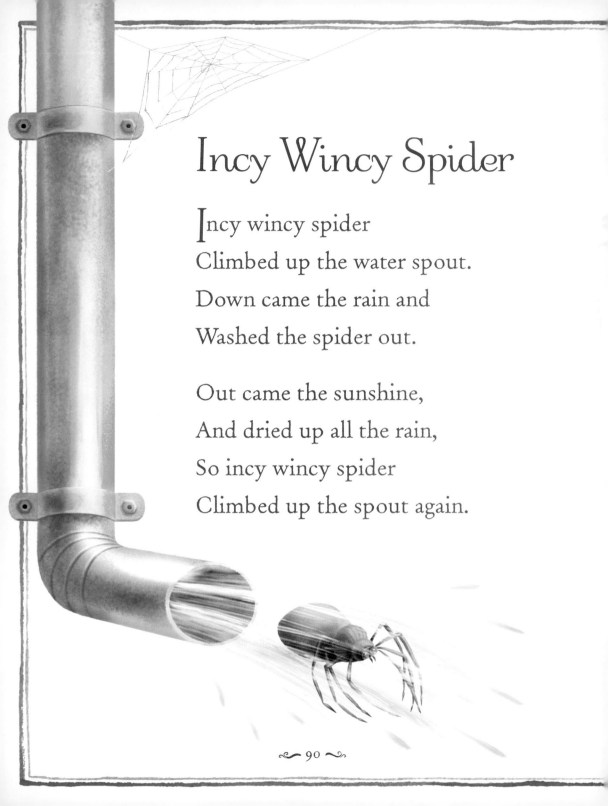

Ladybird, Ladybird

Ladybird, ladybird,
Fly away home,
Your house is on fire,
Your children are gone;

All except one
And her name is Ann
And she crept under
The frying pan.

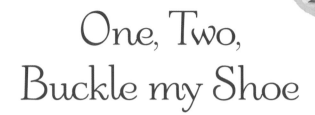

One, Two, Buckle my Shoe

One, two,
Buckle my shoe;
Three, four,
Knock at the door;
Five, six,
Pick up sticks;
Seven, eight,
Lay them straight;
Nine, ten,
A big fat hen;

Eleven, twelve,
Dig and delve;
Thirteen, fourteen,
Maids a-courting;
Fifteen, sixteen,
Maids in the kitchen;
Seventeen, eighteen,
Maids in waiting;
Nineteen, twenty,
My plate's empty.

Tinker, Tailor, Soldier, Sailor

Tinker,

Tailor,

Soldier,

Sailor,

Rich man,

Poor man,

Beggarman,

Thief.

One for Sorrow

One for sorrow, two for joy,
Three for a girl, four for a boy,
Five for silver, six for gold,
Seven for a secret never to be told.

One, Two, Three, Four

One, two, three, four,
Mary at the cottage door;
Five, six, seven, eight,
Eating cherries off a plate.

It's Raining, it's Pouring

It's raining, it's pouring,
The old man is snoring;
He went to bed
And bumped his head
And couldn't get up in the morning.

Rain, Rain,
go away

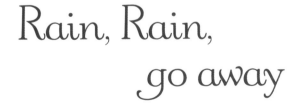

Rain, rain, go away,
Come again another day.

Doctor Foster

Doctor Foster went to Gloucester
In a shower of rain;
He stepped in a puddle,
Right up to his middle,
And never went there again.

The Owl and the Pussy-cat

The Owl and the Pussy-cat went to sea
In a beautiful pea-green boat.
They took some honey, and plenty of money,
Wrapped up in a five-pound note.
The Owl looked up to the stars above,
And sang to a small guitar,
"O lovely Pussy! O Pussy, my love,
What a beautiful pussy you are,
You are,
You are!
What a beautiful pussy you are!"

Pussy said to the Owl, "You elegant fowl!

How charmingly sweet you sing!

O let us be married! Too long we have tarried:

But what shall we do for a ring?"

They sailed away, for a year and a day,

To the land where the Bong-tree grows,

And there in a wood a Piggy-wig stood

With a ring on the end of his nose,

His nose,

His nose,

With a ring on the end of his nose.

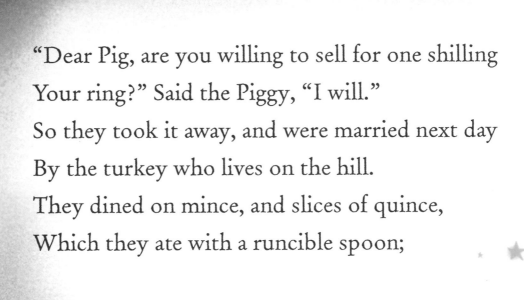

"Dear Pig, are you willing to sell for one shilling
Your ring?" Said the Piggy, "I will."
So they took it away, and were married next day
By the turkey who lives on the hill.
They dined on mince, and slices of quince,
Which they ate with a runcible spoon;

And hand in hand, on the edge of the sand,

They danced by the light of the moon,

The moon,

The moon,

They danced by the light of the moon.

Mother Goose

Cackle, cackle, Mother Goose,
Have you any feathers loose?
Truly have I, pretty fellow,
Half enough to fill a pillow.
Here are quills, take one or two,
And down to make a bed for you.

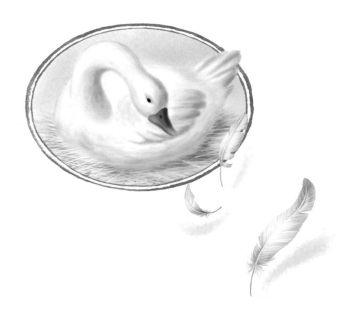

Mary had a Little Lamb

Mary had a little lamb,
Its fleece was white as snow;
And everywhere that Mary went,
The lamb was sure to go.

It followed her to school one day,
That was against the rule;
It made the children laugh and play
To see a lamb at school.

I saw a Ship a-sailing

I saw a ship a-sailing,
A-sailing on the sea,
And oh but it was laden
With pretty things for thee.

There were comfits in the cabin,
And apples in the hold;
The sails were made of silk,
And the masts were all of gold.

The four-and-twenty sailors,
That stood between the decks,
Were four-and-twenty white mice
With chains around their necks.

The captain was a duck
With a packet on his back,
And when the ship began to move
The captain said, "Quack! Quack!"

Pussy-cat, Pussy-cat

Pussy-cat, Pussy-cat, where have you been?
I've been to London to look at the Queen.
Pussy-cat, pussy-cat, what did you there?
I frightened a little mouse under her chair.

I had a Little Nut Tree

I had a little nut tree,
Nothing would it bear,
But a silver nutmeg
And a golden pear.

The King of Spain's daughter
Came to visit me,
And all for the sake
Of my little nut tree.

Bobby Shaftoe

Bobby Shaftoe's gone to sea,
Silver buckles at his knee,
He'll come back and marry me,
Bonny Bobby Shaftoe.

If All the World were Paper

If all the world were paper,

And all the seas were ink,

If all the trees were bread and cheese,

What would we have to drink?

Three Little Kittens

Three little kittens
They lost their mittens
And they began to cry,
"Oh, mother dear,
We sadly fear
Our mittens we have lost."

"What! Lost your mittens,
You naughty kittens!
Then you shall have no pie.
Meeow, meeow, meeow, meeow.
No, you shall have no pie."

The three little kittens,
They found their mittens,
And they began to cry,
"Oh, mother dear,
See here, see here,
Our mittens we have found."

"What! Found your mittens,
You darling kittens!
Then you shall have some pie.
Purr, purr, purr, purr,
Yes, you shall have some pie."

Sleep, Baby, Sleep

Sleep, baby, sleep,
Your father tends the sheep;
Your mother shakes the dreamland tree,
And from it fall sweet dreams for thee;
Sleep, baby, sleep – sleep, baby, sleep.
Sleep, baby, sleep,

The large stars are the sheep;
The little stars are the lambs, I guess,
And the silver moon is the shepherdess;
Sleep, baby, sleep – sleep, baby, sleep.

Rock-a-bye, Baby

Rock-a-bye, baby, on the tree-top,
When the wind blows the cradle with rock.
When the bough breaks the cradle will fall,
Down will come baby, cradle and all.

Hush, Little Baby

Hush, little baby, don't say a word,
Papa's gonna buy you a mockingbird.
If that mockingbird don't sing,
Papa's gonna buy you a diamond ring.
If that diamond ring turns to brass,
Papa's gonna buy you a looking glass.
If that looking glass gets broke,
Papa's gonna buy you a billy goat.

If that billy goat won't pull,

Papa's gonna buy you a cart and bull.

If that cart and bull turn over,

Papa's gonna buy you a dog named Rover.

If that dog named Rover won't bark,

Papa's gonna buy you a horse and cart.

If that horse and cart fall down,

You'll still be the sweetest little baby in town.

So hush, little baby, don't you cry,

'Cause Daddy loves you and so do I.

Girls and Boys

Girls and boys come out to play,
The moon doth shine as bright as day;
Leave your supper and leave your sleep,
And join your playfellows in the street.

Come with a whoop, and come with a call,
Come with a good will or not at all.
Up the ladder and down the wall,
A penny loaf will serve us all.

Wee Willie Winkie

Wee Willie Winkie runs through the town,
Upstairs and downstairs and in his night-gown,
Rapping at the window, crying through the lock,
"Are the children all in bed, for now it's eight o'clock?"

Wynken, Blynken and Nod

Wynken, Blynken and Nod one night,

Sailed off in a wooden shoe,

Sailed on a river of crystal light,

Into a sea of dew.

"Where are you going, and what do you wish?"

The old moon asked the three.

"We have come to fish for the herring fish

That live in this beautiful sea;

Nets of silver and gold have we!"

Said Wynken,

Blynken,

And Nod.

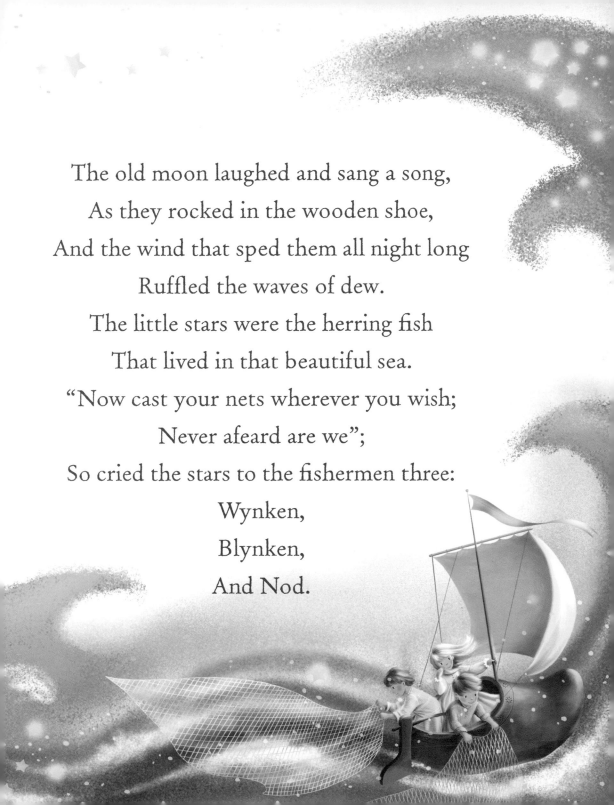

The old moon laughed and sang a song,
As they rocked in the wooden shoe,
And the wind that sped them all night long
Ruffled the waves of dew.
The little stars were the herring fish
That lived in that beautiful sea.
"Now cast your nets wherever you wish;
Never afeard are we";
So cried the stars to the fishermen three:
Wynken,
Blynken,
And Nod.

All night long their nets they threw
To the stars in the twinkling foam,
Then down from the sky came a wooden shoe,
Bringing the fishermen home;
'Twas all so pretty a sail, it seemed
As if it could not be,
And some folk thought 'twas a
Dream they'd dreamed
Of sailing that beautiful sea.
But I shall name you the fishermen three:
Wynken,
Blynken,
And Nod.

Wynken and Blynken are two little eyes,

And Nod is a little head,

And the wooden shoe that sailed the skies,

Is the wee one's trundle-bed.

So shut your eyes while mother sings

Of wonderful sights that be,

And you shall see the beautiful things

As you rock on the misty sea,

Where the old shoe rocked the fishermen three:

Wynken,

Blynken

And Nod.

Twinkle, Twinkle,
Little Star

Twinkle, twinkle, little star,
How I wonder what you are,
Up above the world so high,
Like a diamond in the sky.
Twinkle, twinkle, little star,
How I wonder what you are.

Index

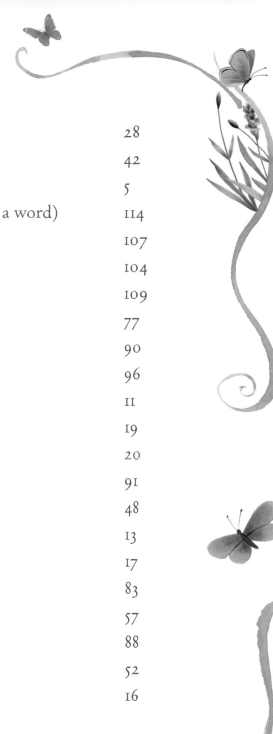

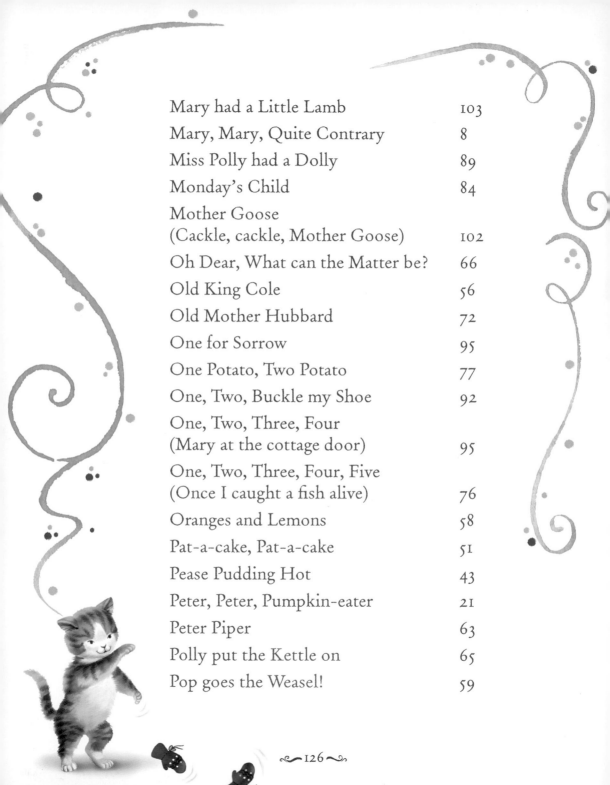

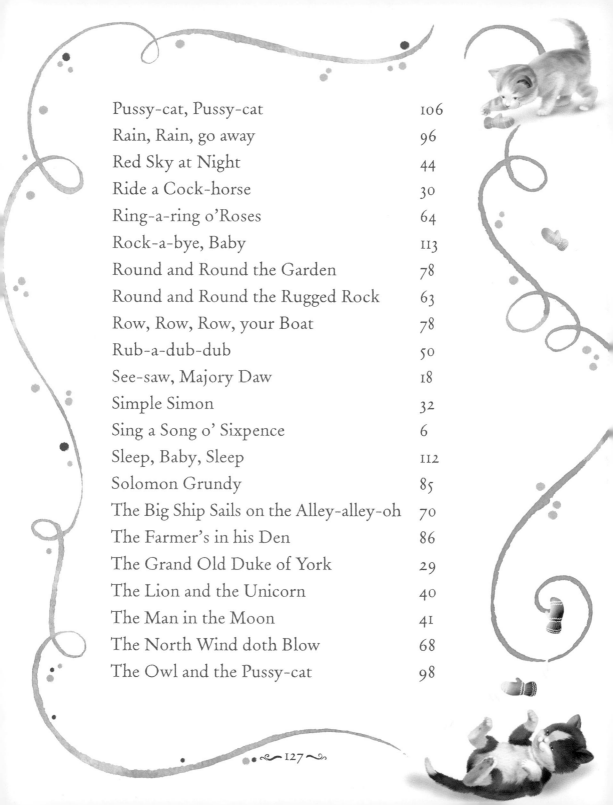

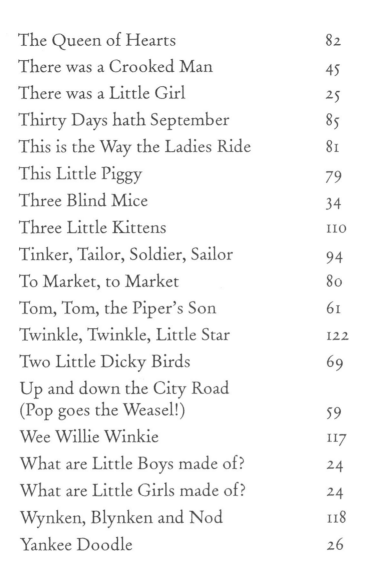

Additional illustration by Katie Lovell. Additional design by Sam Chandler.
Digital imaging by Nick Wakeford. Thanks to Nicola Dickinson for editorial assistance.